SPONSORING
WOMEN

What
Men Need
to Know

By Ida O. Abbott, JD

ONE REALLY GOOD IDEA EVERY DAY
attorneyatwork @

www.attorneyatwork.com

ISBN: 978-0-9895293-1-0

Acknowledgments

Over the last few years, many men have contacted me following presentations or workshops on sponsorship to ask questions or seek advice privately about opposite-sex sponsorship. It was they who gave me the idea for this book. They made me realize that even the most well meaning and supportive men sometimes find it perplexing or problematic to sponsor women, and that while many books, groups and experts tell women to find sponsors, very few resources are available to advise the men who might be those sponsors.

I want to thank the many people who contributed to this book in various ways. They sat for interviews or recommended people for me to interview; they shared stories and experiences; and they offered insights, ideas and useful suggestions about the book's content and production. These individuals include: Andrew Ayre, Raymond Bayley, Katherine Catlos, Kit Chaskin, Howard Coleman, Regine Corrado, Gordon Davidson, Jorge del Calvo, Kerry Francis, Kate Fritz, James Gilliland, James Grayer, Madie Gustafson, Susan Harvey, Lois Haubold, Mark Hutcheson, Natasha Innocenti, Rochelle Karr, David Kremer, Kerri Ann Law, Steve McElfresh, David Miller, Verna Myers, Michael Nannes, Miguel Noyola, Ralph Pais, Lynn Pasahow, Natalie Pierce, Annie Rogaski, Tracy Salisbury, Paul Silverglate, Janet Smith, Nancy Smith, Steve Tarlton, Kari Jensen Thomas, Michael Torpey, Rebecca Torrey, Zack Wasserman, Tammy Webb, Michael Weber and Susan Wilson.

I am grateful to Merrilyn Astin Tarlton, Joan Feldman and Mark Feldman at Attorney at Work for their support and assistance in publishing this book. It has been a total pleasure to work with them.

Most of all, I am indebted to my husband Myles, who has inspired and promoted the careers of so many women and who played a vital role in creating this book.

Ida O. Abbott

About the Author

Ida O. Abbott specializes in developing and retaining professional talent. An expert on mentoring, sponsorship, and leadership, much of her practice is devoted to promoting the advancement of women at work. Ida is a Fellow of the College of Law Practice Management, Co-Founder of the Hastings Leadership Academy for Women, and on the Executive Committee of the National Legal Mentoring Consortium. Prior to starting her consultancy, Ida was a trial lawyer for twenty years. She has held leadership positions in numerous local, national and international professional associations. She is the author of several books and numerous publications, and is a popular speaker at professional meetings, conferences and retreats. Ida's newsletter, *Management Solutions,* can be found on her website, www.IdaAbbott.com.

Contents

PART I

Why Sponsoring Women for Leadership Matters

1

Introduction

Smart business leaders want to be in the forefront of efforts to advance women. As the global economy continues to become more competitive, firms need to use all the talent they can muster — and more and more of that talent will be women. Companies that successfully tap into the full potential of women will be far ahead of their competitors. The key to doing it is to identify women who are likely to succeed and sponsor them so they reach the top levels of leadership. This requires direct personal involvement by leaders, particularly leaders who are men.

Many men who are now or one day will be in a position to sponsor women support gender equity. They are familiar with firm policies and initiatives to counteract gender bias and respect family obligations; they mentor women and participate in firm-sponsored diversity and inclusion programs; and they endorse the principle of treating women fairly and equitably. But few of these men actively champion women, even though they frequently champion other men. Many of them are unaware that they favor men and do not do it deliberately; in fact, they would gladly sponsor women but are unsure how to do it. For other men, opposite-sex sponsorship seems too risky. The potential for "complications," especially those dealing with sexuality, makes them uneasy or unduly cautious. This book offers guidance to those men who want to sponsor women and seek guidance about how to do it, as well as for those who would sponsor women if they could get past their concerns.

Sponsorship Makes the Difference

Sponsorship is critical for women's career advancement. In spite of their high numbers at the entry level and in middle management ranks, women have not been able to break into the higher levels of power and leadership in organizations. Women with the intelligence, talent and drive to be in partnerships and C-suites do not enter the top ranks on a par with similarly qualified men. Considerable research has shown

> Women need the sponsorship of men, and men owe it to women, not because men are to blame but because they are in control. With a near monopoly on power ... men are obligated to ensure that their companies retain and optimize all of the best available talent.

that the reason more men than women get promoted is not because of any inherent differences in ability between the sexes, but because far more men than women enjoy the sponsorship of powerful leaders who help propel their careers upward. This research also shows that when women do have senior-level sponsors, they get promoted at the same rate as men.[1]

Sponsors are powerful backers who identify high performers and actively champion their advancement. Well-placed sponsors can give protégées career-accelerating opportunities and influence decisions about their promotions, clients, and compensation. Because sponsors are by definition powerful, in most organizations the vast majority of sponsors are men. Men hold 86 percent of corporate executive committee positions, 79 percent of senior management positions[2] and 85 percent of law firm equity partnerships.[3] Men make most of the decisions about who gets promoted, how much they are compensated, and how far they advance. Women executives and partners can (and do) also sponsor junior women, but there are too few of them to sponsor the large number of women who aspire to leadership.

Women need the sponsorship of men, and men owe it to women, not because men are to blame but because they are in control. With a near monopoly on power and executive decision making, men are obligated to ensure that their companies retain and optimize all of the best available talent. Otherwise they limit their firms' potential for top performance, growth and innovation. Since women represent half their talent pool, men have the responsibility to create an inclusive, gender-balanced workplace where women can thrive and succeed. They cannot fulfill that duty unless they sponsor more women.

But executives and partners tend to sponsor far more men than women. One major study of sponsorship found that men are 46 percent more likely than women to have powerful backers.[4] This occurs because men have a higher comfort level with men; women do not fit the stereotypical model of what leaders look like; women often hold themselves back and are easier to overlook; and sponsoring a woman raises concerns about sexual affairs, gossip and allegations of harassment.

While it may be easier for men to sponsor other men, they cannot hide behind these excuses to avoid sponsoring women. All of these fears and possibilities are manageable and should not interfere with productive and effective opposite-sex sponsor relationships. Plenty of executive men sponsor women without being deterred by these issues. With more awareness, tools and commitment, men who do hold these concerns can learn to overcome them and sponsor women as readily as they sponsor men.

This book provides the information you need to champion women purposefully and successfully. Part I explains why it is imperative, for organizations as well as for women, for men to sponsor women for leadership. Part II explains how men can sponsor women by offering specific steps for forming and maintaining sponsor relationships with women protégées. Part III addresses issues that men often find particularly disconcerting, and presents concrete suggestions for dealing with feedback, maternity, and sexuality.

Reading this book will make you more aware of why women leaders are vital to your company or firm, why sponsorship is so important to get women into leadership, and the obstacles that impede women's ability to find sponsors. It provides tools to help you develop tactics and strategies for overcoming those obstacles and advocating for the talented women you sponsor. And I hope it will inspire you to commit to sponsoring one or more women right away.

2

Organizations Need
More Women Leaders

Sponsoring women is smart business. Most male leaders today understand how important it is to keep high-performing women in the pipeline and help them achieve their potential within the organization. These men are genuinely concerned about their firms' inability to retain and advance the women they hire because having a substantial number of women leaders is a demonstrably significant benefit to the company, while a lack of gender diversity at the top of organizations can be very costly to the bottom line.

In an increasingly competitive market for talent, retaining the best people and placing them in executive roles where they can have the greatest impact is a business imperative. Abundant research shows that companies with higher percentages of women leaders and senior-level managers tend to outperform their competitors. Studies by numerous organizations have shown repeatedly that having a higher percentage of women in leadership produces quantifiably superior financial results.[5] Here are a few examples:

- Pepperdine researchers found that firms with the best records of putting women into top leadership were 18 to 69 percent more profitable than the median companies in their industries. After studying performance data from Fortune 500 firms over more than two decades, they concluded that, "the correlation between high-level female executives and business success has been consistent and revealing."[6]

- McKinsey research has shown that companies with more women in senior management demonstrated the best financial performance, had 41 percent higher returns on equity, better operating results, and higher growth in stock prices.[7] Companies with three or more women

> Having a substantial number of women leaders is a demonstrably significant benefit to the company, while the lack of gender diversity at the top of organizations can be very costly to the bottom line.

in top positions (on the executive committee or board) scored higher than their peers.[8]

- Catalyst research has found that Fortune 500 companies with three or more women in senior management positions score higher on top measures of organizational excellence. Those companies with the most women board directors outperformed those with the least by at least 16 percent in terms of return on sales and 26 percent in terms of return on invested capital. In addition, companies with three or more women on their boards outperformed the competition on all measures by at least 40 percent.[9]

- Thomson Reuters found that companies with greater gender diversity perform better economically, especially in harsh market conditions.[10]

The Changing Marketplace Demands Women Leaders

Women possess strengths that are critical for leadership in a changing marketplace. Historically, since men were the only players, they designed and created a business world where success was based on masculine traits and behaviors. Women who entered that business environment adopted or at least adapted to masculine behaviors in order to succeed. But the business world is changing, and to operate in the evolving marketplace, the new model of leadership will need to incorporate feminine qualities. Several worldwide studies published in 2013 revealed a growing appreciation for the traits, skills and competencies that are perceived as more feminine, and a strong consensus that those traits are essential to leading in an increasingly social, interdependent and transparent world.[11]

Considerable research shows that additional business advantages accrue to organizations with a substantial number of women leaders. Women executives perform better than men in leadership competencies[12] and they are more creative and effective at problem solving.[13] They are also better able to address clients' expectations because more of those clients are women. Women-owned companies now account for 40 percent of all privately held firms.[14] The number of women-owned companies is growing at a rate one and a half times the national average, and their revenue and employment growth exceeds that of all but the largest publicly traded corporations.[15] In Fortune 500 companies, 22 percent of General Counsel are women.[16] In addition, women are now the sole or primary wage earners in 40 percent of U.S. households.[17] Many of those women are in purchasing roles where they manage, operate and make decisions that place far more value on feminine attributes that were previously undervalued. With an increasingly female client base, a dearth of women leaders and women-led teams deprives a company of perspectives needed to understand and serve women clients.

As an example, women approach decision making differently, so traditional sales techniques may be ineffective with women buyers. Consulting firm Deloitte noted that women executives who make hiring decisions for professional services use different decision-making styles than men. Their internal research found that in sales pitches, partners were using a traditional selling style that was developed when most buyers were men. So, under the auspices of Deloitte's women's initiative, the company taught them selling approaches that take gender differences into account. Whether buyers were men or women, sales results improved when partners were more sensitive to gender diversity and able to adapt to different individual buyers.[18]

As the number of women decision makers continues to grow, this trend will become more apparent and more important. It will have particular impact on law firms and other professional service firms, as more women are in positions to hire and fire outside providers. As the managing partner of a global law firm explained, law firms today want to promote more women to partnership. Clients demand gender-diverse teams; the people who buy legal services are increasingly women who want and expect to hire women; and the competencies necessary for success as a lawyer now include traditionally feminine strengths, such as interpersonal and collaborative skills.

Additional Benefits to Organizations

Organizations with high numbers of women in leadership benefit in other ways that are essential for long-term competitiveness:

- They are better able to satisfy client demands for diverse teams.

- They avoid the high costs of attrition, reaping greater financial returns on their investment in hiring and developing talented women.

- They do not face the problems that women's departures sometimes cause, like annoyed clients, disruption to existing work teams and client relationships, and declining firm morale.

- The presence of successful women leaders makes junior women believe they can succeed at the firm, inspiring them to stay and sustaining their motivation to advance.

The health and prosperity of companies depend on achieving gender balance in firm leadership. Companies where men actively champion women create an environment where women are more likely to achieve higher aspirations, where profitability grows and stays strong, and where the full benefits of gender diversity are more likely to occur.

Benefits to Sponsors

Along with helping their companies, sponsors also benefit personally from championing rising stars. While some sponsors are motivated by altruism or the desire to develop young leaders as part of their legacy, all sponsors receive tangible benefits from their efforts on behalf of protégées. Some of those benefits include:

- The loyalty of emerging leaders

- Access to outstanding performers with top-notch skills who support the sponsor's work

- Allies who can support the sponsor's business and professional goals

- Expansion of the sponsor's network to include influential leaders throughout the organization

- Insights and support from top performers whose skills and talents complement and expand the sponsor's expertise

- Perspectives that differ from the sponsor's, enrich his understanding and expand his thinking

- Information about organizational issues, personnel and operations of which the sponsor may be unaware

- Retention of top performers within the organization

- A reputation as someone who "creates" leaders

3

Sponsorship Is More Than Mentorship

The practice of mentorship is well known and well established in today's workplace. A mentor is someone who helps a more junior person learn, develop and achieve her professional goals. Mentoring is the process by which the mentor and mentee work together to identify and help the mentee move toward those goals. As shown in Table 1 on page 16, mentors serve a variety of roles and functions. Some of these roles support professional development, socialization and confidence building, while others are directed at career advancement. A mentor may serve several of these functions or only one or two, and many mentors who advocate for their mentees eventually become sponsors. Sponsorship can therefore be seen as a set of mentoring functions that are intended specifically to promote an individual's career advancement.

Defining Sponsors and Sponsorship

What we call "sponsorship" today is similar to the old-fashioned notion of mentorship. In the past, a mentor was someone who took you under his wing, shared his wisdom with you, protected you, sent good work your way, introduced you to influential contacts, and generally paved the way for your career success. You were known as the mentor's protégée, which derives from the French word for "protected." The term acknowledged the fact that the mentor had made a personal commitment to you and that your future success was linked to his ongoing support.

As the concept of mentorship has become popularized and programmed, it also has become diluted. Today, mentors are seen primarily as advisors and counselors. They support a mentee's career but do not necessarily go out of their way to promote her advancement. While mentorship remains vitally important for professional development, it is insufficient as a person moves closer to the top where the competition for leadership and partnership are greater and the stakes become higher. At those junctures, what she needs is someone who will be a strong advocate for her — a sponsor, not just a mentor.

A sponsor is an advocate who has power and influence to make his advocacy produce positive career results for the person he is sponsoring — his protégée. He identifies and helps the protégée plan new career moves, helps her develop strategies to move up into new positions, and publicly endorses her. A sponsor takes risks on her behalf, arguing that she should get a bigger pay raise or urging that she is ready for equity partnership or a significant leadership role. He alerts her to opportunities and uses his influence to get her appointed to key posts. He has her back when she takes on new responsibilities, making it safer for her to take risks. He defends and advocates for her behind closed doors when she is not there, and also opens doors and invites her in. Sometimes he calls in favors, puts pressure on colleagues, or puts his reputation and credibility on the line for her.

Specific sponsorship activities are dictated by the unique circumstances of the sponsor and protégée, such as the sponsor's role and range of influence in the company, the protégée's seniority and experience, her career objectives, and the available job openings and opportunities. While the specifics will vary for each sponsor-protégée relationship, Table 2 on page 17 lists some of the things sponsors commonly do for their protégées.

Comparing Mentors to Sponsors

Mentorship may transition seamlessly into sponsorship if the sponsor is in a position of power and believes strongly in the mentee's potential. Mentors may also serve limited sponsorship roles for their mentees. But there are several key distinctions between mentors and sponsors, as described below and summarized in Table 3 on page 18.

Mentorship is supportive, focuses on professional growth and development, and is particularly useful for skills development, socialization, identity formation, emotional support, and personal growth. Sponsorship is predicated on power and focuses on career advancement.

Mentors help people learn how to be reliable and confident performers. Sponsors focus on proven performers, those seen as "stars" or "high potentials."

Mentors are useful throughout your career, especially in the early stages. Sponsors become more important as your career progresses, especially as you near key junctures in your career path or when fewer positions are available, the competition for those limited spots is fierce, and decisions about candidates are not just up to an individual manager.

Mentors can work with several people at once. Sponsors are far more selective; they rarely sponsor more than one or two people at a time.

Mentors can be anyone with more knowledge or experience than you. Sponsors must have sufficient organizational clout to make good things happen for the protégée.

Mentors can be within or outside the organization. Sponsors must be able to influence events within a company or firm, so sponsors are usually found inside the protégée's company. In professional services firms, clients or other powerful outsiders can serve as sponsors because of their ability to influence decisions and practices in the firm.

Although a mentoring relationship depends on mutual trust, mentoring generally involves little risk. Sponsors deliberately take risks on a protégée's behalf and sponsorship therefore demands a great deal of trust. Sponsors trust that protégées will live up to their promise and up to the sponsor's expectations. Similarly, the protégée must trust that the sponsor has her best interests and career goals at heart, the influence to make things happen, and the commitment to follow through.

TABLE 1. COMMON ROLES AND FUNCTIONS OF MENTORS

ROLE	FUNCTION
Host	Welcomes mentee into the organization; Makes introductions, promotes social integration; Provides information about systems, operations and firm culture
Teacher	Teaches technical skills and work processes
Advisor	Advises about work assignments, career decisions, and professional dilemmas; Explains unwritten rules
Facilitator	Helps mentee get good work assignments and make network connections
Protector	Provides cover for risk taking; Runs interference
Coach	Encourages goal setting, monitors performance and progress; Gives feedback; Builds confidence
Role model	Demonstrates appropriate behavior and professionalism
Sounding board	Listens to ideas and plans; Offers reality checks
Confidante	Listens to mentee's doubts, fears and problems; Troubleshoots and consoles
Publicist	Promotes mentee within and outside the firm; Builds mentee's credibility and visibility
Champion	Advocates for mentee's promotion and compensation
Catalyst	Makes things happen; Inspires mentee to act

TABLE 2. SOME ACTIONS SPONSORS TAKE FOR PROTEGEES

ACTIONS
Publicly endorse the protégée's qualifications
Publicly recognize her achievements
Send new business and clients to her
Nominate and support her for promotion or partnership
Introduce her to and foster her relationship with influential people in the firm
Introduce her to and foster her relationship with current and potential clients and contacts
Appoint/nominate her to a leadership position in the firm
Assign her to lead a high-visibility project
Get her a stretch assignment that will spotlight her leadership abilities
Ensure that she gets adequate recognition, credit and compensation for her work
Protect her from unfair criticism
Alert her to new business opportunities
Include her in client pitches and the subsequent work that comes in
Include her/feature her in professional events (e.g., panels, presentations)
Include her/feature her in marketing/business development events
Create marketing/business development events that highlight her interests and talents
Appoint or nominate her for leadership posts in outside organizations
Move her to an office near you or another influential leader

TABLE 3. MENTORS VS. SPONSORS

	MENTOR	SPONSOR
Primary Function	Career support	Career advancement
Experience level of mentee/ protégée	Learner	Proven performer
When assistance is most important	Early and at any time during career	When aiming for promotion or leadership
Number of mentees/ protégées	Several concurrently	One at a time
Qualifications	Anyone who knows more than the mentee	Person with clout
Where found	Anywhere	Usually inside your firm or company
Level of trust required	Moderate	High
Level of risk involved	Low to moderate	High

4

Sponsorship Is Essential for Women to Advance

The benefits of sponsorship are indisputable. Having a highly placed sponsor is a distinct career advantage and when competing for top positions, it can be a critical differentiator. Protégées gain career-enhancing opportunities that others do not get. They receive more chances to excel, are accepted into influential networks, gain visibility as rising stars, and enjoy heightened prestige through the intervention of a powerful backer. They are recognized by others both for their own skillful performance and for having the personal support of a highly regarded sponsor. As word spreads that they are leadership material, their reputation grows and the shared and widespread view of their leadership becomes the "social proof" that makes them *de facto* leaders.[19] This opens still more doors, affords them greater opportunities and increases the likelihood of further advancement.

Sponsorship Is More Powerful than Mentorship

Mentorship is one strategy that has helped women remain in the workforce and make great strides professionally. Mentorship is still important and most women today can find mentors. But without sponsorship, mentoring does not provide the same career benefits for women that it does for men. Both women and men get valuable career advice from mentors, but advice consists of words and good intentions. Sponsorship involves taking purposeful action on another's behalf to advance her career interests, and having sufficient clout to produce results. Sponsorship for high performers occurs regularly in both corporate and professional service environments. However, most of the beneficiaries are men.

Women get advice, while men get promotions ... [M]en's mentors more often serve as sponsors who take an active part in promoting the men's careers, while women's mentors are supportive but do not proactively champion them.

This point was underscored in 2010, when several research studies reported that mentorship gives women fewer career benefits than it gives men.[20] As women and men move through the pipeline, women often remain behind men — even when they have mentors. In short, women get advice, while men get promotions. The reason is that men's mentors more often serve as sponsors who take an active part in promoting the men's careers, while women's mentors are supportive but do not proactively champion them. The studies concluded that without a strong sponsor, women often miss out on promotions, leadership positions, and higher compensation. But when women's mentors are highly placed and take a more active sponsorship role, women are as likely to receive those benefits as men.[21]

Promising women who feel their careers are stalled or thwarted frequently opt to leave the organization. The attrition of women before they reach senior positions is a costly and needless loss of talent. Half or more of the people entering white-collar and professional fields today are women; 53 women are hired for every 47 men. But most of those women do not move into the upper ranks where they can achieve their highest potential. They hold only 37 percent of middle management positions, 28 percent of vice president and senior management roles, and 14 percent of seats on executive committees.[22] In large corporations, at every step up the ladder, men advance at a disproportionate rate, outstripping women nearly two to one. At the topmost rungs of the career ladder, men outnumber women nearly four to one, and at the very top, only 4.2 percent of Fortune 500 CEOs, 4.5 percent of Fortune 1000 CEOs, 14.3 percent of executive officer positions, and 8.1 percent of top earners are women.[23]

Similarly, in law firms, the percentage of women declines dramatically at higher levels. Although women are starting to make gains in new partnership classes,[24] they remain underrepresented at every tier of leadership and influence. The higher up you look, the smaller the percentage of women you find. Women represent half of new law firm associates but compose only 15 percent of equity partners (a ratio which has not changed significantly for 20 years) and 4 percent of firm chairs or managing partners.[25] Even at the 50 law firms recognized as "best for women," women represent just 19 percent of equity partners and 22 percent of executive committee members. Moreover, rainmaking is a key to being even considered for law firm leadership. Very few women rank among the top rainmakers in law firms; 22 percent of the 50 best firms have no women at all among their top 10 rainmakers.[26]

The gender gap shows up in compensation as well as in leadership positions in corporations and law firms. The gap between men and women's compensation is dramatic and gets worse for women at executive levels, even on corporate boards and among law firm equity partners.[27] From entry level to management positions, women continue to earn 23 percent less than men for the same work, and the gap is widening. Even the highest paid women corporate leaders earn an average take-home salary roughly 18 percent less than their male peers,[28] and women General Counsel and Chief Legal Officers earn 21 percent less than men in the same jobs.[29] In law firms, male partners on average make approximately 30 percent more than female partners, even when they bill the same hours and have comparable books of business.[30] The pay gap between women and men cannot be explained by performance, productivity, or any factors other than discriminatory practices.[31]

The same pattern is especially pronounced in science, technology, engineering and mathematics (STEM) fields. Although women hold 41 percent of corporate STEM jobs in the entry and lower levels, half of those women drop out of their profession.[32] Women in STEM jobs earn 14 percent less than their male counterparts, even after controlling for other factors, such as age, education and area of specialization.[33] Women in these fields start out as gifted and motivated as men, but they leave because of a culture that offers them little encouragement or positive reinforcement. Instead, they are underappreciated, undervalued and isolated, face extreme work pressures, and encounter roadblocks at every turn. And they lack sponsors who could counter these negative forces.

Sponsors are especially critical for women of color, who face stereotypes and biases both as women and as members of racial and ethnic minority groups. But they, too, are often ignored by the power brokers who could help them. White professionals are 63 percent more likely to have sponsors than professionals of color.[34]

Many women of color come from and have been shaped by vastly different economic, social, immigrant and cultural circumstances than the majority of people with whom they work. Many are the first in their families to have college, much less graduate, degrees. These women have to contend with "intersectionality," which refers to discriminatory experiences that result from having multiple identities (e.g., race, gender, ethnicity, immigration status, and class) and cannot be explained by any one identity alone.

Women of color need not prove just their ability and career commitment as women but must also overcome coworkers', supervisors' and clients' negative assumptions and biases based on their race or ethnicity. They find their accomplishments ignored and their mistakes exaggerated; they are denied desirable assignments and meaningful feedback; they are deprived of access to leaders, clients and development opportunities; and they are excluded from informal firm networks and marginalized in formal ones. They may be celebrated publicly for recruiting or business development purposes as evidence of the firm's diversity but passed over internally for important projects or promotions. At work they are often the only minority woman or part of a small group of others like them. With few people in the organization to whom they can fully relate or who can relate to them, they feel isolated, alienated and second class. Having a sponsor who believes in, protects and advocates for them can counteract these negative factors, build their confidence and help them envision and achieve career success.

Actions Speak Louder than Words

It is no longer sufficient for men simply to voice their support for women. Men in leadership must act with resolve to ensure that these invisible barriers are eliminated and that women receive the same career-expanding experiences, opportunities and support that are widely available to men. Men cannot expect women to correct the situation by themselves. With so little representation in the inner circles, women do not have enough power to drive the changes that are necessary to make firms more equitable; but men do. And there is one thing that all male leaders can do, individually, toward that end: they can sponsor women.

Sponsorship is not by itself a solution to the dearth of women in leadership or the gender gap in pay, but it does start to level the playing field when women have powerful sponsors as readily as men do. While most organizations say they make gender diversity a priority, women remain skeptical because they see few women at the top and few men taking action to change the situation. Building trust and confidence in the firm's commitment is essential to keep women engaged and in the pipeline, heading toward leadership. Men who sponsor women make a strong, personal and public statement that they are committed to gender equity — and doing something about it.

5

Why a Man Might Not Pick a Woman As a Protégée

Let's assume a powerful man works with two junior colleagues, a man and a woman, who are both equally talented, motivated, and superbly skilled performers. According to what we know from research and experience, that powerful man is more likely to sponsor the man than the woman. Why is that? What factors go into a sponsor's calculation about where to place his most active support and for whom to expend his political capital? And why don't more women come across as "leadership material," even when their talents and abilities should make them great candidates?

Stereotypes, Mixed Signals, and Sex

One reason why men do not recognize women as candidates for sponsorship centers on the fact that ambitious women are trying to be leaders in a world where the model of leadership is predominantly male. When a man looks for leadership potential, the automatic favorite is someone who looks and acts the way leaders are supposed to – which usually means another man. When a woman aspires to top positions, she is out of sync with the way women are expected to act. Those expectations about women are based on stereotypes about what women think, want and do. They are the product of socialization as we grow up in our families and communities, and they are embedded in the norms of the places where we work. They color our attitudes and beliefs even though we may be completely unaware of it. Sometimes those deep-seated but unconscious expectations and attitudes actually contradict what we consciously think. Nonetheless, these unconscious biases impact our judgments and decisions about people. When the norm for women is to be collegial and nurturing, a woman who is more autonomous and professional may be suspect. She may be a high achiever who does first rate work, but lingering biases about women cast doubt on whether she has what it takes to be a leader.

Another reason that many women are not obvious protégées is that their behavior does not send a definite signal that they want to move into leadership. A woman may have a great deal of skill and a high work ethic but without some clear outward signs, the sponsor may question whether she has the ambition, drive, focus, or political smarts to operate at an executive level. Women are not usually as direct about their ambitions as men are, do not advocate for themselves as openly as men do, and believe that they should be judged and promoted on the basis of merit, not by using politics and influential connections. If being a leader means changing these attitudes and behaviors, and if changing means being inauthentic, women may become ambivalent about leadership. This sends confusing signals to men in positions to promote them. Based on what they see — and don't see — in women's behavior, potential sponsors may assume women are not interested in executive roles.

A third reason has to do with sex. Men are sometimes reluctant to enter into a sponsor relationship with younger women because of possible sexual tensions or misperceptions — their own and others'. They worry that people will spread rumors, spouses will become jealous or that misunderstandings could lead to allegations of harassment. Rather than run any risks, they give their attention and support to men and avoid sponsoring women.

Even when a sponsor does not harbor these biases or worries, he has to persuade other people who do. One woman told me her sponsor expressed his frustration after he successfully led the way to having her named a partner in her firm. She was the first woman he had ever sponsored and, he told her, "You'll be the last one. I've never had such a hard time sponsoring a man. People gave me pushback on things no one had ever raised before." It was fortunate for this woman that her sponsor persevered, but problematic for other ambitious women that he was so discouraged. It would have been easier for him if he had appreciated the unfair obstacles that make it hard for women to get promoted. Then, instead of giving up on women, he could be better prepared to deal with the challenges.

Understanding the reasons why women do not get sponsored and the obstacles they face can help men acknowledge women who have the ability and drive to get ahead and warrant a sponsor's support to help them get there — but who might otherwise be overlooked. With greater awareness, men can then:

1. Prevent their biases from controlling their decisions, and prevent the biases of others from controlling the outcomes;

2. Recognize and sponsor women who place unnecessary limits on themselves; and

3. Manage any sexual concerns they may have about sponsoring a woman.

Let's look into each of these issues in greater detail.

1. The harmful impact of gender bias on women's careers

Gender bias reflects entrenched beliefs and assumptions about women based on stereotypes about appropriate roles and behaviors for women. Unconscious thoughts about the kinds of work women are and are not suited for, especially if they are mothers, remove highly qualified women from consideration for leadership opportunities and positions. In the past, working women suffered overt discrimination and explicit bias. They were told outright they were not "fit" for certain jobs, were too emotional and unreliable to be given responsible roles, and were taking the place of men who needed to support families. Sometimes the bias was ostensibly intended to "protect" women and occasionally it was hostile. But it was out in the open and women understood the barriers they faced.

For the most part, women no longer experience this kind of explicit bias. But the underlying thoughts and stereotypes that support gender bias have not gone away. They remain underground, in the subconscious where people may not realize they hold the thoughts at all.[35]

In a recent study, researchers at Yale found that scientists at six major research institutions, when presented with resumes that were identical except for their names (John and Jennifer), viewed the male applicant more favorably than the woman, were significantly more likely to offer the man a job and career mentoring, and set his salary at $4,000 higher than the woman's.[36] The scientists' unconscious bias led them to judge the man more competent and more worthy of support than the *identically qualified* woman.

This "second-generation gender bias" is subtle and often invisible but it is firmly embedded in "cultural assumptions and organizational structures, practices, and patterns of interaction that inadvertently benefit men while putting women at a disadvantage."[37] This unspoken but potent bias in favor of men is not deliberately intended to harm women. But when leaders make judgments and decisions based on inaccurate and biased assumptions, they give men unfair advantages although they may not realize it.

Unconscious gender bias plays out in many ways. The effects of gender stereotypes about the ambitions of men and women provide a good illustration. Sponsors look for individuals who are strong performers and hungry to succeed. But women who want to reach the top face a dilemma. Having openly high career ambitions is expected for men. It is a hallmark of masculinity. But many people believe women are not — or should not be — ambitious. So, women with the same aspirations as men are judged harshly because they seem unfeminine and unnatural. Assertively reaching for the top goes against the norm that women in our society should be modest. When women who want to move up the career ladder advocate for themselves in order to make their accomplishments and aspirations known, they are criticized for being braggarts, "overly ambitious" or "self-important." To be safe, many women keep their ambitions to themselves — which makes them appear less ambitious to potential sponsors.

Even when the evidence is to the contrary, many people cling to the belief that women are less ambitious and place lower priority on their careers. In fact, young women in business and law are as openly ambitious as men are early in their careers.[38] Recent studies from the Pew Foundation[39] found that young women today value career success more than men: "Two-thirds (66%) of young women ages 18 to 34 rate career high on their list of life priorities, compared with 59% of young men." Among people aged 35 to 64 who said "being successful in a high-paying career or profession" was very important to them, the percentage of women and men was the same (42 percent and 43 percent, respectively). Mid-level women and men share a strong desire to advance to the next role and women aspire to be CEOs in equal proportions to men.[40] Yet when women try to get ahead using the same career advancement strategies as men, even when they do "all the right things," they earn less and progress more slowly than men.[41] What happens?

As they move along, men receive more career-enhancing assignments than women do.[42] Men have work that involves larger budgets and more staff, higher visibility, greater client contact and other work experiences that give them more attention from the C-suite or partnership. They are appointed to committees and roles that deal with money, growth and strategy, while women are more frequently appointed to those that involve people and administration, which are less powerful and less valued. Men are invited to client pitches and business development activities while women are left to find clients on their own. Men are offered career-advancing international posts more frequently than women because it is assumed men will be freer and more willing to take them than women — especially married women — would be.

Men receive these advantages in large part because they are assumed to be ambitious and suited for leadership. At the same time, however, women are deprived of opportunities and resources that might draw attention to their leadership aspirations and abilities. So sponsors help propel men into positions of power and perpetuate the status quo, while women have to fend for themselves. The lack of sponsorship further impedes women's progress, disheartening women and reinforcing the mistaken belief that they lack ambition.

This inaccurate belief can become a self-fulfilling prophecy. Watching men with lesser credentials, ability or experience being offered better opportunities and moving higher in the organization convinces women that the odds of advancing to executive levels are stacked against them. Despite their confidence and desire to advance, women do not receive the encouragement and support to reach for the top that men do, and they come up against barriers that discourage them and raise doubts about whether the struggle to get there is worth it. When almost all leaders are men, men on the rise can assume success is a possibility. Women cannot. When they see few or no women role models, are not offered important business opportunities, are excluded from informal networks, and do not have anyone who champions their success, women feel they need to be exceptional to get ahead, and even if they are, the chances are slim. In these circumstances, some women may respond — not unreasonably — by lowering their ambitions or leaving their jobs.[43]

This pattern was reflected in the 2013 American Lawyer Midlevel Associate Survey.[44] The survey found that midlevel women law firm associates were less likely than men to see themselves as future law firm partners. Although law firms say they are committed to gender diversity, these women see few women partners or leaders, fewer still who have children, and an unspoken "motherhood penalty" for women who do. They are less satisfied than men with the level of responsibility they are given, receive less client contact than men, and do not see a clear path to partnership. Despite various programs and initiatives to support women, women remain skeptical as to whether their firms are truly committed to promoting them. To the contrary, they perceive that law firm partners are looking for clones of themselves. Accordingly, they doubt that they can become partners and are more likely to leave.

Other common patterns of gender bias include holding women to higher standards than men, expressing contradictory expectations ("double binds") for women, and exhibiting "maternal wall" bias, which leads people to believe that women with children are unable to meet the demands of leadership.

Different standards: People expect more of women than of men and they hold women to higher standards. This sets the bar higher for women who aspire to leadership and makes it more difficult for them to prove their value to the organization, even though research shows that women outperform men in 17 of 67 critical leadership skills, while men outperform women in only four.[45]

People also judge women and men differently: women on their performance and men on their potential. For example, where a man and woman have spent the same time and effort pursuing a sale that did not materialize, some will say the man "just needs more time" while the woman "has not produced." He is given the benefit of the doubt while the woman must prove her ability over and over again. Similarly, when men succeed, it is assumed that they did so on their merit ("he landed that client because he worked hard"), while a woman's success is attributed to external factors ("she got the business because the client wanted to hire a woman"). Conversely, when men fail, external factors are blamed ("he has too much work"), but women's failings are attributed to their own inadequacies ("she's disorganized").

The subtle but direct harm of these different standards was shown in a study of law firm associate performance evaluations at a Wall Street law firm. The study found that women received more positive comments (e.g., "excellent," "stellar," "terrific") than men, but only 6 percent of women — as opposed to 15 percent of men — were mentioned as potential partner material. What's more, women who received the same narrative comments as men about their technical competence and partnership material nonetheless received lower numerical ratings than men. Because the firm relied on numerical ratings for partnership consideration, men in the firm were three times more likely than women to be promoted to partnership even when women exhibited the same performance, competence and partnership potential.[46]

The implications of "potential vs. performance" create a decisive advantage for men who are considered for promotions, since the principal issue under consideration is the candidate's perceived potential for success in the higher role. It also makes men more appealing candidates to sponsors who are banking on a protégé's likely success in the future. This leaves women toiling away without the benefits of sponsorship or access to the best opportunities, and it slows down their career progress.

Double binds: Double binds are situations where you cannot win no matter what you do. Women leaders face a classic double bind. In our business culture, leadership and masculinity are closely linked. Men fit seamlessly into leadership roles because gender is not an issue for them; leadership is presumed to be masculine. But gender is a salient factor for women leaders because they stand out as different from the prevailing norm, which is male. Men are expected to be forthright, ambitious, assertive and independent (to "take charge"), while women are expected to be nice, nurturing and communal (to "take care"). So how should a woman leader behave?

When a woman in authority exhibits behaviors traditionally considered feminine, she is seen as "too soft" to be a leader and is not respected as competent. But if a woman leader is self-confident and competitive or pushes her team hard to perform, she is perceived as "too tough," which makes her unlikable. In either case, when high-achieving women act and succeed in ways that violate gender stereotypes, the very behaviors that create their success contravene social expectations about how women are supposed to behave. Deviation in either direction can lead to backlash, penalizing women for their success.[47] In contrast, men do not face this trade-off between competence and likeability; for men, the two are positively correlated. Indeed, men benefit from exhibiting a "softer side."

In this environment, women whose abilities are demonstrated in ways that are not conventionally masculine — by being collaborative rather than directive, or responsive rather than assertive — may be dismissed as candidates because the importance of those strengths for a leader are unappreciated. This sends aspiring women leaders the message that being anything other than a traditional leader is a liability; that senior women who have adapted to the traditional model are not credible mentors or role models; and that authentic leadership for women in the organization is unattainable, undesirable, or both. To a potential sponsor, this makes men more appealing protégés than equally qualified women because their behavioral norms are clearly understood and established, and sponsoring them is less complicated or controversial.

Maternal wall bias: People assume that women with children are less committed to their work. This bias arises from the stereotypes that create conflicting expectations for mothers and career women: good mothers should always be available to their children, while good business people should always be available to their clients. Maternal wall bias calls into question the leadership qualifications of pregnant women and mothers, subjects them to unfavorable treatment at work, and interferes with their ability to advance. It also deprives them of sponsorship, as sponsors save their support for people they can rely on without question. Having a sponsor, however, can keep working mothers engaged and on an upward trajectory. Research by the Center for Talent Innovation found that 85 percent of full-time employed mothers with sponsors remain on track compared to only 58 percent of those without sponsors.[48]

A lot of sponsorship development takes place after work or outside the workplace. Sponsor relationships usually evolve over time as two people get to know each other on a more personal level and the sponsor sees that the junior person's personality, values, and career goals are compatible with his. In developing sponsor relationships, fathers have an advantage over mothers in at least two ways.

First, most men find it easier to participate in these outside activities than women do. Men with families have fewer obligations at home, where wives still perform most of the caretaking and household chores. It is easier for these men to work late hours, travel to meetings, attend client events on short notice and go out for a drink with the boss after work. This gives them more time to start and cultivate relationships with sponsors. This imbalance is changing, slowly, as many young men now try to be equal partners to their wives in caring for home and family, but for the most part, working mothers still have more home-centered obligations than fathers do, which reduces their time for getting to know sponsors.

Second, even mothers who do not feel constrained by domestic responsibilities are excluded from many sponsor-developing activities. Sponsors assume that mothers cannot or prefer not to spend time with them outside work; do not have the time to work late, travel at the last minute or spend time schmoozing; and cannot concentrate fully on their work or their careers. As a result, women with children are frequently passed over for high-quality work, assignments that require travel or relocation, job promotions and business development opportunities. With the best of intentions, leaders do not ask mothers to consider projects or assignments that may be great for their careers but may be tough to carry out. The reasons may be benign — to save the mother from too many work demands at the expense of her family — but the impact is to slow her progress regardless of her ambitions. If she has a sponsor, he could speak up for her and make sure she gets access to high-powered work, but her chances of having a sponsor are dimmed by the belief that she is not sufficiently committed to her career or able to carry out her responsibilities.

A potential sponsor usually looks
for someone who is self-confident
and ambitious to get ahead. …
The reluctance of women to promote
themselves and express their
ambitions makes them less visible
to potential sponsors.

2. Women hold themselves back

Many women are uncomfortable calling attention to their achievements
and ambitions, dislike politics, have difficulty asking others for a career
boost, or underestimate the importance of powerful backers. This
makes it harder for potential sponsors to recognize how worthy these
women are of their support.

Some women hurt their own chances for sponsorship by failing to let
sponsors know what they want and why they merit it. Sponsors are
drawn to star performers who display confidence and a drive to succeed. Where a man might insist he is the right person for a job and ask
to be promoted, a woman who is equally or even better qualified may
downplay her qualifications for the job. Instead of aggressively pursuing promotions and opportunities, she waits to be asked, and then,
when asked, may turn the offer down. She may prefer to keep doing
her current job, which she finds meaningful; she may have family or
other outside commitments that conflict with the demands of the new
position; she may undervalue her qualifications; or she may fear she is
not ready and see the promotion as too great a risk. Regardless of the
reason, she does not project the kind of go-getter image that captures
the notice of sponsors.

A potential sponsor usually looks for someone who is self-confident and ambitious to get ahead. He wants to know that a protégée wants to be a mover and shaker in the field, a partner in the firm, or a leader in the organization. The sponsor is making an investment and wants a high return, so he must be assured that the protégée has both star power and staying power. While some sponsors might inquire about a woman's career goals, most expect a would-be protégée to make them known. They want to support someone who is already making people see her as a leader, displaying confidence and seeking opportunities to show what she can do. The reluctance of women to promote themselves and express their ambitions makes them less visible to potential sponsors.

Women also are averse to leveraging relationships or "playing politics" to move ahead. They find the use (or even the concept) of deal making and political maneuvering "dirty" and discomfiting. Yet people who are politically astute are more likely to get ahead because organizations are political places.[49] Wherever there are competing interests that need to be resolved — for example, a limited number of partnership slots or committee positions — people try to influence the outcomes of decisions and allocations. That process is political. Some workplaces are less political than others, but political considerations are rarely absent altogether.

Women believe that people should be judged and promoted on the basis of performance, and that getting ahead based on "who you know" is unseemly and unfair. Organizations pride themselves on being meritocracies, so women take them at their word and focus principally on putting in their hours and doing good work. They fail to realize that even in meritocracies, it is the people in power who decide what is deemed meritorious, how merit is defined, and the relative value of different categories of merit. Their decisions are not purely objective. Personal interests and competition for firm resources and personnel color their decisions and trigger political action.

Women who reject politics fail to see that building and leveraging relationships with powerful figures is not just a means to secure power for selfish reasons, it is the very exercise of leadership. Leadership is a process of influencing people to produce positive outcomes for the firm.[50] As you move higher in an organization, success becomes less about what you do yourself and more about what you can achieve through others. A leader must be able to build consensus, create and use alliances, acquire resources, execute plans and persuade people to work together in pursuit of shared goals. Whether to achieve her personal goals or the company's business objectives, she must be able to cajole, call in favors, apply pressure, trade promises, and use other political techniques to reconcile the competing interests of others. A leader must demonstrate that she can do these things before others will accept her as a leader.

A sponsor can make the protégée realize it is not just palatable but admirable to be politically savvy by reframing the process in a way that emphasizes the positive leadership aspects of politics. He can work with her to develop a leadership style that makes effective use of political techniques but is also honest, open, and authentic. By helping her learn to navigate the political dynamics of the organization constructively, he can make her a better leader.

Networking issues: Related to women's aversion to politics is their limited appreciation of how their networks can help them get ahead professionally. Developing strong business networks is critical for career advancement. Because a leader operates through others, her value and effectiveness are largely tied to the power of her network. Yet women are reluctant to cultivate potential sponsors through their networks, while men willingly use patronage and networks to open doors and provide opportunities that cannot be accessed through normal channels. Men attribute their promotions to personal connections as a matter of pride, not embarrassment, because it means that influential people see them as leaders and reward them accordingly. As a result, men benefit from the political processes that go on all around them while women lose out.

The quality of the relationships in an individual's network can determine how quickly and how high that person rises. In business, network relationships are based on the principle of reciprocity, that if you do something for someone they will return the favor. We hear it in many common sayings, such as "One good turn deserves another." This principle has a social basis and is found in virtually all societies because it facilitates transactions among individuals and across time when people feel obligated to repay what they have received.[51] Reciprocity is not a direct quid pro quo exchange; it creates no specific expectation but rather a diffuse generalized obligation.

Yet many women view reciprocity as an objectionable basis for relationships; they feel that relationships should be social and "relational," not transactional. They believe that helping others should be an end in itself, not the basis for an exchange of favors; they feel that trading on one's relationships is crass. While they have no trouble calling in favors to help others, these women are squeamish about asking friends for work or career assistance because it would blur the line between friendship and business. They don't want friends to feel they are being used.

Most men see no such boundaries between business and friendship and have no such hesitation. Trading favors shows they are in the game; it builds their reputation as someone who can do things for others and deserves their support in return. Thus they are able to use their network relationships more effectively to attract both business and sponsors, which smoothes the way for them to move up.

Power issues: Similarly, many women do not recognize the importance of having a sponsor who is powerful. They do not appreciate the vital role that power plays in career advancement. They associate power with manipulation, exploitation or corruption, and fail to see that they need power to get things done, influence change and have an impact. They do not see how necessary power is — both their own power and that of their allies and supporters — to becoming a leader and being an effective one. Instead of looking for sponsors who can wield power on their behalf, they are drawn to people who offer support, advice, and role models to emulate, even when those individuals do not have the influence or ability to make a positive difference in their careers. Consequently, women fail to pursue relationships with powerful men who may not be especially supportive, sensitive, or good role models, but who are best positioned to help them move ahead.

For women who place these constraints on their careers, sponsorship can make an enormous difference. It can embolden them, build their confidence and increase their determination to succeed. By giving a high-performing woman the public recognition she deserves for her mastery, providing chances to prove her leadership ability and encouraging her to pursue others, helping her become more politically savvy, and showing her how to leverage her network relationships to help her reach positions where she can help others as well as herself, a sponsor can sustain or rekindle a woman's ambitions and inspire her to fulfill them.

3. Women, men and sex

A close work relationship between a man and a woman can generate sexual tensions in one or both of them. When the man is older and powerful and the woman is young and ambitious, the potential for complications is even greater. Even when the relationship is strictly business focused, it can be the subject of rumors, gossip and speculation among coworkers, and it can arouse feelings of jealousy and resentment in the sponsor's wife. Men also worry that innocent comments or actions — theirs or the protégée's — might be misunderstood, embarrassing or even actionable. Rather than deal with these risks, men sometimes avoid sponsoring women, deliberately or without even realizing they are doing it.

These are not irrational or unjustifiable worries. The problem is that they conflict with a leader's responsibility to develop and promote talented individuals irrespective of gender. When men let these fears stop them from sponsoring women because of their sex, they are engaging in discrimination and holding women back.[52]

Rather than yield to such fears, executive men can fulfill their sponsorship responsibilities to women while abstaining from sexual entanglements, averting public misperceptions, maintaining marital harmony, and avoiding accusations of harassment. This requires understanding the issues involved, exhibiting a high degree of self-awareness and self-control, and displaying sensitivity, clear-headedness and professionalism.

These issues are discussed below; specific advice for how to address them is provided in Part III: "Dealing With Feedback, Flexible Schedules, Parenting Leave, Family Obligations and Concerns About Sex."

Sexuality. Sponsorship can be very intense, involving a strong connection that is personal as well as professional. When a man sponsors a woman, the relationship sometimes stirs up sexual feelings in one or both of the individuals. And occasionally those feelings may lead to intimate relationships.

The fear of an illicit sexual liaison — even the fear of being *suspected* of having one — inhibits opposite-sex sponsorship. One study of sponsorship found that 64 percent of senior men avoid one-on-one contact with junior women. This is not a concern restricted to men; the study also found that 50 percent of junior women are reluctant to have such contact with senior men,[53] and, in fact, the career penalties of illicit relationships are significantly greater and longer lasting for junior women than for senior men.[54] When the relationship changes from professional to romantic, it may tarnish the man's reputation, but it puts the protégée's future in jeopardy. Moreover, the scandal can spread a fear of opposite-sex sponsorship throughout the office and make it harder for other men and women to have sponsor-protégée relationships.

A risk of romantic entanglement is real. Research data from the same sponsorship study found that more than one third of the executive women surveyed admitted to having an affair with their boss or knew another woman who did.[55] The risk looms particularly large when a powerful senior man and an aspiring junior woman work together in an intense relationship that requires spending time together alone and discussing personal ambitions, needs and desires. Even though their focus is on work and career, sponsor and protégée might very well become sexually attracted to each other. One law firm partner was quoted in an article as saying, "You spend time with a young woman who looks up to you, and you feel flattered, and before you know it, one thing leads to another ... Things happen."[56] The attraction may be momentary or it may grow into something more serious and long term.

It goes without saying that sponsor and protégée should always behave professionally. They should avoid highly intimate settings and sexually provocative banter. They should steer clear of situations that are overly intimate and interactions that may arouse sexual feelings. They should establish clear guidelines and boundaries. While people may not be able to stop the feelings that are stirred, they can stop themselves from acting on them. Self-control is not easy but it is imperative.

As one man I interviewed said, "To sponsor women, it's important to have a happy marriage." There's no doubt that a trusting and secure wife can make it easier for a man to support the careers of other women.

Gossip and rumors. Relationships in the workplace are frequently the subject of rumors, and close relationships between senior men and junior women are tasty fodder for the gossip mill. Because sponsorship between a man and woman is not as common as sponsorship between two men, it is more noticeable and subjects the man and woman to greater scrutiny. Rumors can spread even in the most innocent situations, but they can be especially rampant in offices where affairs between senior men and junior women have been known to occur. In a workplace where it has happened in the past, suspicions of impropriety are common and not unreasonable. But they can taint blameless people unfairly and hurt them professionally as well as personally.

People may spread rumors about a male sponsor and his female protégée and speculate that the nature of their relationship embraces more than work. Whether just trivial gossip or malicious in nature, the impact can be harmful to both parties. It sullies their reputations, disparages their credibility, and undermines their integrity. For a woman rumored to be "sleeping her way to the top," it casts doubt on her competence and ability, suggesting that the real reason for her advancement is sexual, not professional. In some cases it can foreclose opportunities completely, as others are reluctant to be alone with her or work with her at all, for fear of being tainted or ensnared, or because they question her ability or judgment.

Although they do not have to explain or justify their relationship to others at work, it is important for both sponsor and protégée to be aware that this can happen and to behave professionally at all times. If either sponsor or protégée is worried about others' misperceptions or believes that people are talking about them, they should raise the issue and discuss it together. They may need to adjust their behavior toward each other, change their activities or take other appropriate action to reinforce publicly the solely professional nature of their relationship.

Spousal jealousy. Wives sometimes become jealous when their husbands have close relationships with women at work. When their wives get angry, accusatory or emotional, these men may find it difficult to take women to evening client meetings or on business trips, or even just to work late hours at the office with a woman. This makes it hard enough for them to engage with women on work teams, but putting in the additional time and effort that sponsorship entails presents particularly tough challenges. So some men refuse to take women to lunch, social events or other activities where being together might suggest even a hint of impropriety. Some women face similar problems with jealous husbands and find it easier to turn down assignments and invitations from a senior man rather than risk a confrontation at home. Whether it is his jealous spouse or her jealous husband, this marital stress deprives women of the chance to spend time with men who might want to sponsor them.

As one man I interviewed said, "To sponsor women, it's important to have a happy marriage." There's no doubt that a trusting and secure wife can make it easier for a man to support the careers of other women. But not every marriage is happy and not every wife feels secure. Even a wife who does trust her husband may worry when he spends a lot of time in close contact with a talented and ambitious woman, especially if she is young and attractive.

Harassment. The laws against sex discrimination and harassment have done a great deal to protect women from abusive treatment at work. Many companies require attendance at programs that caution men to avoid any behaviors or situations that might lead to an accusation of sexual harassment. These preventive efforts have been widely effective but they also have made men wary of situations that might give the impression they engaged in inappropriate comments or conduct. Men worry that a woman might misinterpret an innocent statement or move; that they might misconstrue a woman's behavior as a come-on and make a misstep in response; or that a woman might use the law as a weapon to manipulate them or take revenge if she becomes angry. An allegation of harassment, even if proven to be untrue, can taint a man's reputation, hurt his career and make his life miserable.

These sex-related concerns lead some men to restrict their dealings with women at work. They insist on leaving the door open when they are alone with a woman in an office or conference room; they refuse to take a woman to lunch alone; they will not travel with women on business trips. The impact of these restrictions is detrimental to women. All relationships, but especially sponsorship, require trust and a personal bond; removing the possibility of a private conversation inhibits the formation of a personal relationship. Spending time together is how people get to know each other's values, character and career aspirations. Avoiding any degree of closeness means that any relationship that does form will remain superficial.

Depriving a woman of these relationships and of experiences such as business-related travel has numerous discriminatory and deleterious effects on her career. She has fewer opportunities for high-profile, career-promoting projects and is excluded from meetings, networks and events where other important relationships could be formed. Clients may become suspicious, wondering if the woman's office-bound role means she is less capable or responsible than the men who come to call. At the same time, the men whom senior men do sponsor, and who are invited to lunch, business trips and client events, enjoy tremendous advantages that come from being included.

PART II

How Men Can Successfully Sponsor Women for Leadership

6

Establishing a Sponsor-Protégée Relationship

Essential Elements of Sponsorship

Most leaders engage in sponsorship and have been sponsored themselves, so the nature of a sponsor-protégée relationship should be familiar. Generally speaking, you sponsor women just as you do men. You may have to make a little more effort up front, and you might need to adapt to the impact of motherhood and other sex-related differences, but the strategies and tactics that sponsors use to help women move ahead are not much different than those for men.

The cornerstones of sponsorship are

• Trust

• Mutual Commitment

• Open Communication

In a successful sponsor relationship, both parties feel they have the trust of the other, that each is being honest, and that each will be loyal. They admire and respect each other as people and professionals. They know they can depend on each other and that each will try everything possible to protect the other's interests and not to let the other down. They agree on what they want to achieve, even if they sometimes disagree on certain issues or tactics. They feel comfortable speaking their minds and openly communicate their expectations, aspirations, perspectives,

In deciding whether to sponsor a woman, you might be inclined to favor a protégée who is much like you. But you may find greater benefit in sponsoring someone who has different strengths, views and styles.

doubts and concerns. These elements are important for most healthy relationships, but they are essential for sponsorship to thrive.

Some organizations have formal sponsorship programs where leaders are asked to sponsor a particular protégée. Those programs usually have stated expectations, guidelines and objectives for participants.[57] Even in formal programs, however, the sponsor-protégée relationship cannot be imposed. A sponsor must trust, believe in and desire to further the career of an up-and-coming woman leader, and the woman must earn that trust and support from a potential sponsor. Programs that formalize existing relationships or pair up leaders with high-performing women they already know and admire stand a good chance of success. Programs that match people who must start their relationship from scratch require: more time for relationship and trust building; opportunities for the sponsor to work with the protégée or see her in action; substantial ongoing support; and sponsors who are strongly motivated to make the arrangement succeed.

Three Ways to Initiate Informal Sponsorship

Most sponsorship occurs informally, without any structured or programmatic context. Informal sponsor-protégée relationships usually start in one of three ways.

The most common way is when a senior manager or partner identifies someone as a star performer, believes that she has what it takes to succeed, and wants to make that success happen. The sponsor recognizes her talent and potential while they work together or when he observes her at work and is impressed by her ability. As the two work together their relationship grows. They develop mutual trust and respect, both as professional colleagues and as individuals. They might not have the same political or religious beliefs and they may lead very different social and home lives, but they share common values around work and client service. Frequently, but not always, they become close personal friends.

Sometimes, though, a senior leader might be impressed by the quality of a woman's work and believe she could be a major asset to his practice or the company, but he does not know her well enough to know whether she has what it takes to become an executive. He checks with colleagues who have worked more closely with her, and based on what they tell him, he feels she may be a good candidate for sponsorship. Nonetheless, he still needs to find out for himself whether she is someone on whom he wants to spend his political capital. He needs to be sure of her career ambitions and whether they are in sync with his business vision and plan. He wants to know if she has had any significant leadership experience or if she wants such experience. These are things he needs to find out directly from her.

A third way that sponsorship is initiated is when a woman asks a man to be her sponsor. But leaders do not enter into such relationships casually. Before a man can even consider it, he should ask her for a specific proposal for help, and have her make the case for why he should agree to it. The would-be sponsor will want to find out enough about both her and her proposal to make an informed decision. If he knows her well this may be very straightforward. But if he does not know her well or has reservations, he will want to do some due diligence before making a decision.

No matter how the relationship is initiated, before you become a sponsor, you should feel confident that the would-be protégée is ready and motivated to move ahead, that she's the right person for you to sponsor, and that you are enthusiastic about helping her. In deciding whether to sponsor a woman, you might be inclined to favor a protégée who is much like you. But you may find greater benefit in sponsoring someone who has different strengths, views and styles. Relationships are enriched when parties complement each other. You should both share similar values but have abilities in different areas and diverse perspectives. Finding ways to turn differences into advantages can enhance the relationship, strengthen the protégée's career prospects and demonstrate your leadership in promoting an inclusive firm culture.

Confirm Your Choice Through Conversations

If you have any hesitation about sponsoring a particular woman, initiate conversations to gather more information from her. Enter those conversations with an open mind and without preconceived ideas about her ambition or commitment. Approach her with genuine interest and curiosity, ask open-ended questions, and invite her to question you as well. It is important for both of you to develop rapport, get to know each other better and start to develop trust. During your conversations, be sensitive to any discomfort or anxiety she might feel, and stress your business and professional reasons for thinking about sponsoring her. In the course of these dialogues you can:

- Tell her directly that you think she has the potential to move up and would like to know more about her career interests and aspirations.

- Ask about her past experience and the kind of leadership experience she wants in the future.

- Share your own story and career history, including past experiences as both a sponsor and a protégé.

- Ask if she has outside commitments that might be impediments. If she says yes, explore strategies that could accommodate both her outside obligations and her desire to advance at work.

- Explain the kind of career assistance you can offer her and what you would expect from her, and ask her if she wants your help.

In these dialogues, you might discover that a potential protégée may not have considered becoming an executive or even seeking a promotion. You might need to help her envision herself in a higher role. If she has doubts or uncertainties, address them. Explain the characteristics that you believe make her an excellent candidate and how the firm will benefit from her leadership.

Some women who are outstanding candidates for sponsorship may feel conflicted about accepting your proffered support, especially if they have priorities or obligations that conflict with the demands of leadership. For example, the timing may be inopportune. A woman with young children might not want to move into a higher level of management at the time you bring it up to her. But priorities change over time, so try to determine if the woman wants to forego the promotion completely or simply delay until a later date. Discuss with her the pros and cons of putting it off — especially if the opportunity is unlikely to occur again — and also whether you will be open to sponsoring her when she feels ready. If you feel strongly that she should take the opportunity now, explore various options and try to help her find a way to reconcile her priorities with the leadership possibilities you are presenting.

7

How to Effectively Sponsor a Woman

When you sponsor a woman, there are many steps that you can take to ensure that the relationship is productive and achieves its objectives. Below are some tips for getting off to a strong start and following through effectively, especially by focusing on career opportunities and promoting your protégée to others.

Early in the Process

• **Ask her how you can help.** The protégée might have some specific ideas in mind. Ask her how you can best help her to be successful and what she hopes to gain from your support.

• **Clarify the purpose and goals of your relationship.** If you or your protégée has a specific position or goal in mind, make it clear. If not, discuss what successful career outcomes might look like.

• **Develop a strategy.** Use your knowledge of advancement paths within the firm to analyze her current status, what she needs (e.g., skills, experience, contacts) to move toward her goals, how she will obtain them, and how you will help her. Work with her to produce a vision of success, a plan of action and tactical means for making her vision a reality.

• **Be clear about what you expect of her.** Sponsors may support a protégée just for the satisfaction of helping her move ahead in her career. However, if you expect something more specific from your protégée, such as taking on some of your responsibilities or serving as your voice on a committee, discuss it with her to see if she agrees.

- **Explain how to get ahead — including the unwritten rules.** When the criteria for advancement are explicit, you can plan with them in mind. Even if they are explicit, analyze with your protégée the political and other unstated factors that will have to be managed in order to get her ahead. If she is uncomfortable dealing with the political dynamics, explain why a leader needs to be able to operate within a political arena and offer her ideas about how she can engage in the process with greater comfort while maintaining her integrity and authenticity.

- **Be open with your protégée.** Let her see you as a whole person, including your professional weak spots. This will make her feel more comfortable opening up to you and sets the stage for trust to grow.

Throughout the Relationship

- **Be honest.** In order to be honest and direct with each other, you both must feel free to speak your mind. Tell your protégée to speak up if she ever feels you are being unfair, harsh or out of place and let her know you will do the same if you feel she is out of line. Recognize that comments or actions may be misinterpreted. Agree that before jumping to conclusions, you will give each other the benefit of the doubt.

- **Inform her.** Share information about company strategy, how the organization operates, firm economics, team and department dynamics and other data that will expand her understanding of the business and the people running it.

- **Prime her for leadership.** Help her envision herself as a leader. When she sees herself as a leader she is more likely to behave in ways that cause others to view and treat her as one. This will give her greater influence and impact and in turn, reinforce her self-perceived leadership status.

- **Invite her into important networks.** When you and some other powerful colleagues get together informally, invite your protégée along. If you are a member of influential organizations, professional societies and social clubs, take her to meetings and events, and introduce her to other members. Include her in conversations and if necessary, make others comfortable with having her there.

• **Help her find an effective leadership style.** It is essential for your protégée to find a leadership style that suits her. The way she approaches a leadership task or problem may be very different from the way you or other leaders in the firm would do it. Her style does not need to conform to any prevailing model of leadership; the key question is whether it works for her and produces the desired results. Help your protégée develop a style that is both bold and authentic. Discuss characteristics and styles of good leaders you both know and which ones might be effective for her. Let her practice various approaches with you. Observe her at work and give her feedback about her impact on others.

• **Encourage her to stretch.** Your protégée may feel insecure or unprepared to assume greater risk, visibility or responsibility. Tell her why you feel she is capable and ready to stretch her horizons; give her specific reasons. Emphasize the new skills she will acquire in the job, and assure her that you will help her learn what she needs to know to be successful in her new role. Give her tips to mitigate the risks she perceives.

• **Support her when she assumes new roles.** You have a personal stake in your protégée's success. As she assumes new roles or responsibilities, teach her how to anticipate and deal with the challenges they bring. Give her tips on how to get through difficult situations. Sometimes she may run into problems. If she has trouble in her job — or after her next promotion — be there to help her figure out what the problem is and how to deal with it.

• **Anticipate and prepare for unpleasant situations.** Sometimes your protégée will find herself in tough or unpleasant situations. If you expect that an upcoming event may be difficult for her, discuss it with her in advance so she can be ready to handle it. For example, she may have to meet with a group of client representatives who tell off-color jokes, use bad language or do other things that your protégée might consider impolite or offensive. Before the meeting, ask if she wants to be treated like "one of the guys" and put up with it, if she wants you to ask them to behave better when meeting with her, or if she wants to handle it her own way. Explore the pros and cons of each approach.

• **If she is a woman of color, acknowledge and help her navigate gender and race concerns.** If you are sponsoring a woman from a racial or ethnic minority group, be sensitive to how her gender and race or ethnicity might cause her to feel isolated and like an outsider, even though she has achieved a significant degree of professional success. She might need guidance in how to overcome subtle expressions of bias, such as being left out of important projects, networks or business development opportunities because co-workers or clients stereotype her, feel uncomfortable or lack affinity toward her. Or she might need you to give her reality checks to help her figure out if offensive comments or behaviors are due to racial hostility or ignorance, or if they are slights at all. If they are intended as slurs she may want your advice about how to deal with them. If you sense that these kinds of concerns are problems for your protégée, tell her that you are available to talk with her about them if and when she ever wants to talk. Let her know that you will try to help her as much as you can. She might not want to confide in you but it is important to let her know you are open to it if she does. If you or she thinks someone else, perhaps a woman leader of color, might be better able to help her, suggest someone you know or encourage her to seek someone out on her own. If you are a man who is also a member of a minority group, you may find it relatively easy to discuss your shared minority status, but you still need to consider how her experiences as a woman differ from yours and help her address gender-related concerns.

• **Maintain perspective.** Some sponsors push their protégées hard. Hard-charging sponsors can help emerging leaders become more resilient, but they can also depress their confidence, drain them of energy, or even drive them to the breaking point. It is important to recognize when you might be pushing too hard and need to back off.

• **Pay attention.** Listen carefully to your protégée and observe her attentively. Even in a close relationship, people find it difficult to discuss some things. If you sense she is worried about something but does not say anything about it, ask her and let her know she can safely talk with you about it if she wants to.

Focus on Career Opportunities

• **Identify the assignments critical for advancement.** In every organization, some kinds of projects and work assignments are essential for advancement. These jobs offer knowledge and insight into the firm's operations, sources of revenue and business strategy. They expose an emerging leader to key decision makers and clients. Make it a priority for your protégée to get these critical assignments.

• **Help her learn to judge the value of opportunities.** Your protégée might not see the long-term benefits of some assignments or she might overestimate the value of others. Help her recognize which projects, committees, client relationships and leadership positions will be beneficial to her — and also those which will not. Watch out for "gender traps": assignments that tend to be given to women but are not likely to advance your protégée's career. In a corporation it might be staff positions rather than line jobs; in a law firm it might be the training committee rather than the finance committee.

• **Find her a niche.** In many organizations, advancement requires specialized expertise. Help your protégée find an area in which she can distinguish and differentiate herself.

• **Focus on opportunities to showcase her strengths.** Look for opportunities that will allow her to use her talents and expand her visibility. If she prefers collaboration to competition, find projects where she can showcase the value of her approach. If she has outstanding interpersonal skills, find projects that will give her a chance to demonstrate them. Let others see her succeed.

• **Urge your protégée to seek out opportunities.** Encourage her to volunteer for or otherwise go after any vital career-enhancing opportunities she learns about. Urge her to seek election or appointment to leadership in professional and community organizations and on non-profit boards. Offer help and advice if she has any questions about the opportunities she is considering.

Help her recognize which projects, committees, client relationships and leadership positions will be beneficial to her — and also those which will not.

• **Be on the lookout for opportunities for your protégée.** When you become aware of new work, projects or client needs that would be good for her, send them her way. Recommend her for prominent speaking engagements, client pitches or leadership development programs.

• **Create opportunities for your protégée.** If you are setting up a strategy committee, chairing a national conference or wooing a potential client, give her a prominent role. When you are asked to speak to an important gathering, ask her to help you prepare and to attend with you. At the event, invite her to share the stage and give her credit for her contributions.

• **Let her decide.** Do not assume that your protégée will want to accept the assignments or opportunities you find for her. Ask her if she is interested in them. Listen to her reasons. If she says no but you feel it is important for her career, you can try to persuade her and find ways to make it more appealing and workable for her. But the decision is ultimately hers.

Promote Your Protégée to Others

• **Advocate for your protégée privately and publicly.** When you are in meetings with senior managers, partners and decision makers where personnel are discussed, praise your protégée to colleagues or clients by emphasizing her professional accomplishments and future potential. If a project or business opportunity is under discussion, assert the reasons why your protégée is the best person for the job. During compensation discussions, make sure the compensation committee knows why she deserves a big pay raise or bonus. Nominate her for important, high-visibility roles inside the firm and in professional or civic organizations, and lobby to get her appointed or elected.

- **Build a support base.** There's no need for you to work alone on your protégée's behalf. Gather allies and build a consensus about her star power. Get other leaders vested in her success and enlist their help in getting her great opportunities and raising her profile.

- **Make use of succession planning and elections.** If your company has a succession planning process for leadership positions or for taking charge of client relationships, or holds elections for significant management roles, encourage your protégée to throw her hat in the ring for those that will advance her career. Recommend her for them and strongly voice your support to key decision makers.

- **Transition your clients to her.** If you are at a point in your career where you are thinking about handing off clients or key business relationships to another professional, prepare your protégée to take them over. Help her build a relationship with the client and over time, help the client become accustomed to dealing with her as your successor.

- **Call in favors.** If you see a project or assignment that will be an important platform for your protégée, call in favors with the people in charge if necessary to get it for her.

- **Protect her from bias.** Watch for signs of bias in others that might cause people to judge your protégée by stricter standards than men, reduce her opportunities, or otherwise diminish her prospects. Make sure she is a meaningful member, not just a token, on project and client teams. Speak up on her behalf if you believe she is unfairly criticized or subjected to gender bias. If criticism from others makes her doubt herself, help her rebuild her confidence.

- **Make sure your protégée is compensated fairly.** Help her prepare for annual compensation discussions and for negotiations regarding promotion-related compensation. Urge her to keep track of her accomplishments and describe her capabilities, and help her present them in a way that proves her worth. Offer to practice with her if she expects the negotiations to be difficult or she finds it hard to advocate for herself. Speak up for her to decision makers and ensure that they are not making false or biased assumptions that might impact their award. Be especially alert if your protégée works reduced hours, takes family-related leave or makes use of other work-life policies. Firm policies may set a formula that protects base pay, but bonuses or other discretionary forms of compensation may be negatively affected by gender bias.

• **Address naysayers.** If others challenge your support for this protégée, explain why you support her and why they should too. Present the business case for your support and tell them you will be held accountable if she fails. If anyone tries to sabotage her success, confront him or her directly.

• **Tell stories about your sponsorship experience.** As a leader, your personal commitment gives credibility to the value of sponsorship generally and the merits of your protégée in particular. Telling stories about your protégée's successes can influence others to view her as a leader. Stories about your sponsorship experience and the benefits you derive from it can also serve as a model for other sponsors and inspire them to sponsor women.

Learn from Your Experience

• **As you work with your protégée, learn from her.** She is a source of valuable feedback for you about your personal style and how others perceive you. She can fill you in on what is happening in the organization that you may not know about. As you listen to her perspectives, observations and experience, consider new ways you might think and act and new approaches you might take with your colleagues, clients and career. And as she progresses, relish her success. Take satisfaction, professionally and personally, in her achievements.

• **When she achieves her career goals, let her go.** Some sponsors expect protégées to show their gratitude by remaining in the sponsor's thrall long after they are promoted. But as protégées become high-ranking leaders, they also become their sponsors' peers and may even surpass them. Be prepared and excited to see your protégée move ahead.

PART III

Dealing With Feedback, Flexible Schedules, Parenting Leave, Family Obligations and Concerns About Sex

8

Give Your Protégée Feedback

Feedback is important at any level of professional development. For a woman trying to become a leader, honest, clear and practical feedback is essential. She needs to know both how well she is performing and how to project the image she wants others to have of her. You can let her know by providing timely information, concrete suggestions and supportive guidance. Be truthful and tactful; do not sugarcoat the message, but keep it focused on what she needs to do to get ahead. In every feedback conversation, make your message concise and clear, and concentrate on the career implications of the feedback you give her.

Men often withhold feedback from women because it makes them uneasy. They fear that raising certain subjects might be perceived as harassment. They worry that they might inadvertently hurt a woman's feelings or cause her to become emotional. But sponsors cannot hold back important messages that can make a difference in a protégée's career. After all, you are trying to advance that career and your reputation is tied to her success.

You are in a position to give her feedback that others cannot or will not give. If you have established a trust-based relationship with her, you should be able to talk with your protégée about subjects that would otherwise make one or both of you uncomfortable.

When giving your protégée feedback, explain why you are bringing it up. Point out why her current approach is not effective; give specific examples you have observed. Emphasize the need for colleagues, clients and senior executives to have positive perceptions of her and how your advice will help her look and act like a leader. Make sure she understands your message and what she needs to do.

Examples of Sensitive Feedback Issues

Presence. If your protégée lacks executive presence, let her know. Leaders must have presence; that is, a confident demeanor and bearing that attracts attention and respect. They must project gravitas without seeming distant or detached. If your protégée needs to appear more authoritative, explain that listening carefully, speaking up appropriately and communicating confidently will show people her competence. If she is timid, has poor posture, does not project her voice, or does not make eye contact, explain that engaging others through eye contact, an erect stance, a friendly facial expression and open body language shows them that she is interested in them and welcomes people to connect with her.

Communication. Similarly, if her communication skills are not as good as they should be, point out some specific issues she should work on. For example, some women like to process their thoughts verbally. When meeting with clients or colleagues, they laboriously explore pros, cons and different possibilities before reaching a conclusion. The conclusion may be brilliant, but a busy executive or client who just wants to hear the bottom line may perceive her as unfocused, indecisive and wasting his time. Let her know this is a problem so she can correct it.

Appearance. A particularly sensitive but important area for feedback is the protégée's personal style, manner and appearance. Appearances matter and your protégée needs to know it. Dressing inappropriately or unattractively projects a poor image and may impact her credibility as a leader. Ask her to think about the kind of impression she wants to make on people who will be judging her — and whose judgments will impact her success. If she wants to be seen as a leader, she needs to be taken seriously and come across as professional and thoughtful about her appearance. She can have a distinctive fashion style; it just needs to suit the situation. In the executive suite, courtroom or boardroom, her fashion preference should not get in the way of what she wants to accomplish.

Before talking with her about how she looks, dresses or carries herself, consider whether your assessment is based on your personal preference or on evidence that it is ineffective in promoting her work, reputation or career. When it comes to style and appearance, there is usually more than one "right" way. Make sure that you are not expecting her to conform to a traditional model that might be outdated or unsuitable for her. Her approach might be unconventional but, perhaps with some fine-tuning, it might be effective for her.

Also consider the double bind she may face:

- Women are told to "look good but not too good," to look feminine but not too feminine, to be attractive but downplay their sexuality, to remain modest but stand out.

- Many women like to use makeup and wear clothing that looks professional yet also conspicuous and attractive. But when they do, managers may not take them seriously or give them important work.

- African American, Hispanic and other women of color are told to be authentic but also advised to conform to white norms of dress in order to fit in.

These contradictory messages create confusion and can make feedback about appearance difficult to hear, especially from a man.

It also makes it tricky for men to give women feedback about these sensitive issues. You may have enough confidence and expertise to provide adequate feedback and advice about them, or you may feel out of your depth. If so, admit it and suggest that another colleague or a professional might be able to help her more than you can. For example, if you think she would benefit from a voice coach or fashion consultant, encourage her to find one or offer to ask your contacts for recommendations.

9

Dealing with Flexible Schedules, Parenting Leave and Family Obligations

A talented, ambitious woman who works less than full time or takes extended family leave is extremely vulnerable to being derailed professionally. Whether because she is "out of sight/out of mind," or because people doubt her commitment, she may be disregarded for promotions or high-profile projects. A sponsor can ensure that she has access to those opportunities and support when she accepts them. He can make the difference between this woman staying on track and ascending to top leadership posts or leaving the company for another job.

Because some people may use the protégée's part-time status or temporary leave to challenge her capacity for leadership, it is important for the sponsor to defend her. Accentuate her current achievements and long-term value to the firm. If people resist working with her because of her reduced hours or outside commitments, articulate why the benefits of helping her achieve her potential outweigh any inconvenience they may feel in accommodating her schedule.

There are many ways to support her scheduling needs without significant burden to her team. If team leaders are willing to give it a chance, they can assuredly make it work.

Prove that it can be done by modeling it yourself. Show that you and your team can be flexible without resenting any inconvenience it might cause. Let your protégée know you will back her as she tries to fulfill career, work and family obligations, and back up your assurances with action.

If your protégée takes a family-related leave, encourage her to develop a plan for ramping off before the leave begins and ramping back on when it ends. Throughout her leave and when she returns, protect her from others who might give up on her because they believe she has lost focus, ability or commitment to work. When she returns, make sure she continues to get good work commensurate with her ability and aspirations.

Whatever her schedule restrictions are, discuss them together. Consider client needs and expectations, project deadlines, management responsibilities, and other office demands, as well as your own time constraints. If she cannot attend meetings at certain times, if she works from home some days, or if she wants to have phone meetings in the evenings after her kids are in bed, try to work out reasonable alternatives and come up with a plan that works for both of you.

10

Concerns Related to Sex

If you are concerned about the possibility of sex-related problems, consider the degree of risk involved and whether you are willing to assume it. Before you decide, consider first that you might be exaggerating the risk, and second that this is a risk that can be prevented and managed. Some men use these concerns as rationalizations to avoid sponsoring women for other reasons. Don't be one of them.

Here are some suggestions to prevent sexual entanglements, rumors, spousal jealousy and allegations of harassment:

- Act professionally at all times.

- Avoid or limit alcohol when you and your protégée are together.

- Set boundaries, either explicitly or through your actions. Consider it your "personal code of behavior." Make it known that you have a policy not to date coworkers. Clear boundaries are important whether you and your protégée are married or single.

- If you are unsure about her boundaries, ask her. Emphasize that you do not want her to feel uncomfortable around you. Urge her to let you know if you ever do anything that makes her uncomfortable so that you can stop doing it.

- Honor your protégée's boundaries (e.g., if she has a "no-hugs" policy).

- Avoid stories or jokes about sexual topics or that have sexual overtones.

- Do not assume your protégée finds you sexually attractive. If you are attracted to her, do not assume the feeling is mutual.

- Exercise self-control. One or both of you may in fact be attracted to the other. Temptation is powerful and very human, but it can be resisted.

- Apply a presumption of innocence. Assume that whatever your protégée tells you, including information about her personal life, is within your relationship as professional colleagues and friends, nothing more.

- When discussing personal matters, curtail conversations that start to stray into topics that may become sexually charged. Topics that seem innocent and natural between friends, such as complaints about your spouse or hers, can lead to unexpected entanglements between professional colleagues. Talking about being lonely, unhappy or needing comfort may inadvertently lead to physical intimacy. If the discussion is necessary (e.g., one of you is going through a divorce that is affecting your work or concentration), tread carefully.

- Spend your time together in public places and during the day. Unless an evening or weekend meeting is necessary, meet during breakfast, lunch or breaks during the workday.

- When you need a private place to talk, opt for offices, conference rooms, restaurants or other venues where you can be seen but not heard.

- Participate together in office, professional, civic, cultural and athletic activities that give you a chance to connect on a personal level but where safe boundaries can be maintained.

- Introduce your protégée to your wife. Encourage them to get to know each other. Invite the protégée and her husband or partner to your home or a restaurant for dinner so both spouses can get acquainted and witness the professionalism of your relationship. Use firm social events as opportunities for all of you to spend time together. If either or both of you have young children, include them in some activities.

Some men have wives who get jealous or resentful when their husbands sponsor young women. If you have a strong marriage and a secure wife, explain your sponsorship intentions to her so that she understands and accepts the situation. If you have a shaky marriage or an insecure wife, the problem is harder to deal with, and it may be intractable if your wife's suspicions are because you have had affairs or given her reason to be jealous in the past. Your wife's personal problems and your need to repair relations with her have to be addressed, perhaps through counseling, but that is outside the scope of this book.

As a sponsor, you need to be aware of how your personal problems may interfere with your professional responsibilities and deal with them as best you can. What you should not do is run away from those problems by limiting your sponsorship to men. That would be a violation of your obligation as a leader to ensure that your firm has the best talent in place to guide and ensure its success.

It is also important to recognize that you are not alone in your concern about sponsorship with the opposite sex. Women also refrain from seeking male sponsors for the same reasons. Women are more comfortable with women mentors and sponsors, are afraid of becoming the subject of scandal or salacious rumors, and have husbands and partners who may become jealous of the attentions of an older successful man.

If your protégée is married or has a partner, acknowledge his role in promoting her success. Let her know that you consider him a partner in your effort to help her advance because his support for her is essential to that endeavor. When appropriate, for example, if she receives a promotion or award, contact him and recognize both her accomplishments and his support for her.

If you sense that your protégée has any concerns or problems because of your sponsorship, ask her about it. Tell her you are willing to address them. If she declines, respect her choice but let her know you will remain open to talking about it at a later date. If she does present any sex-related issues, deal with them directly and honestly, and try to work out an arrangement that will make her feel safe.

Conclusion

Sponsorship is a personal undertaking. A man who sponsors a woman takes it upon himself to advance her career. He puts his reputation on the line for her and tells the world she is worth it. She still has to earn that promotion, but his solid, public vote of confidence — and the power he puts behind it — at least gives her a fair chance to get it. In return, sponsors receive personal satisfaction and capable and loyal leaders who help them achieve their business goals and build their legacy.

Companies have numerous gender diversity programs and initiatives designed to help women generally. As important as those programs are, they are not enough to produce gender-balanced leadership. To create a truly inclusive workplace, these initiatives must be coupled with cultural change. Gender bias is ingrained in institutional norms and systems. Its elimination requires a firm-wide change effort, which is both a company responsibility and, for leaders, a personal one.

The changes necessary for gender balance will happen only when enough courageous men get personally vested in helping women succeed. This is why sponsorship plays such an important role. Sponsors have far-reaching impact on an organization's culture. They are role models for other senior leaders, reminding them that achieving more diverse leadership starts with purposeful individual action. They disprove gender biases by showcasing strong, ambitious, successful women and giving them a chance to soar. They are paragons of leadership who ensure the ongoing health and vitality of the firm by creating its future leaders. In these ways, sponsors serve as catalysts for the cultural transformation needed to make gender balance a reality.

APPENDIX

A. Men Sponsoring Women: Taking a Personal Inventory

Your past experience with a sponsor

Think of someone who did something to help advance your career.

What did they do to help you?

Why did they want to see you advance? What was it about you?

What was the impact on your career?

How did it make you feel about your career?

How did it make you feel about your company/firm?

Your past experience as a sponsor

Whom have you sponsored in the last five years?

What do those people have in common?

In what ways are they different?

How many were women?

If you have not sponsored any women during the last five years:

Were there any women you could have sponsored during this period?

Why did you not sponsor any women?

Were your reasons based on assumptions or facts?

How can you manage, counteract or eliminate those reasons?

If you have sponsored one or more women,

In what ways, if any, did it differ from sponsoring a man?

Did you encounter any difficulties related to your being opposite sexes? If so, how did you deal with them?

What did you and your protégée do to make the relationship successful?

What was the outcome?

What did you learn from the experience?

How did you benefit? How did she benefit?

In retrospect, would you have done anything differently?

B. Preparing to Sponsor a Woman

Think about five or six women with whom you have worked, or whom you have observed at work, over the last year who have made a strong positive impression on you. Select one you would like to sponsor.

How well do you know this woman? What do you know about her background, work experience, current work situation, career goals and ambitions?

What more do you need to know to facilitate your sponsorship?

How will you obtain the information you need? What will you ask her? What information will you obtain from other sources?

What do you see as her particular strengths and talents?

In what ways do you think you can help her?

What obstacles do you see that might interfere with your ability to sponsor her? How will you overcome them?

How will you let her know you are interested in sponsoring her?

What will you expect from her? How will you tell her?

NOTES

1 Sylvia Ann Hewlett, *(Forget a Mentor) Find a Sponsor* (Boston: Harvard Business Review Press, 2013); Heather Foust-Cummings, Sarah Dinolfo and Jennifer Kohler, "Sponsoring Women to Success," Catalyst Research, August 2011, http://www.catalyst.org/knowledge/sponsoring-women-success; Nancy M. Carter and Christine Silva, "Mentoring: Necessary But Insufficient for Advancement," Catalyst Research , December 2010, http://www.catalyst.org/knowledge/mentoring-necessary-insufficient-advancement.

2 "Women in Senior Management: Setting the Stage for Growth," Grant Thornton International Business Report, 2013, http://www.gti.org/files/ibr2013_wib_report_final.pdf (women represent 21 percent of senior management in North America, 24 percent globally); Joanna Barsh and Lareina Yee, "Unlocking the Full Potential of Women in the US Economy," McKinsey & Company Research, April 2011, http://www.mckinsey.com/client_service/organization/latest_thinking/unlocking_the_full_potential.

3 "Report of the Seventh Annual NAWL National Survey on Retention and Promotion of Women in Law Firms," The National Association of Women Lawyers and The NAWL Foundation, October 2012, http://www.nawlfoundation.org/pav/docs/surveys/NAWL%202012%20Survey%20Report%20final.pdf

4 Sylvia Ann Hewlett, with Kerrie Peraino, Laura Sherbin and Karen Sumberg, "The Sponsor Effect: Breaking Through the Last Glass Ceiling," Harvard Business Review Research, December 2010, http://genderprinciples.org/resource_files/The_Sponsor_Effect.pdf.

5 E.g., Barsh and Yee, "Unlocking the Full Potential of Women in the US Economy," supra; "Girls Allowed: How a Renewed Focus on Culture Can Break the Diversity Stalemate," PA Consulting Group, 2013, http://www.paconsulting.com/our-thinking/girls-allowed-how-a-renewed-focus-on-culture-can-break-the-diversity-stalemate/; David Gaddis Ross, "When Women Rank High, Firms Profit," Columbia Ideas at Work, June 13, 2008, http://www8.gsb.columbia.edu/ideas-at-work/publication/560/when-women-rank-high-firms-profit.

6 Roy D. Adler, "Profit, Thy Name Is ... Woman?" *Pacific Standard,* February 27, 2009, http://www.psmag.com/business-economics/profit-thy-name-is-woman-3920/.

7   "Women Matter: Making the Breakthrough," McKinsey & Company Research, 2012, http://www.mckinsey.com/client_service/organization/latest_thinking/women_matter; "Women Matter: Women at the Top of Corporations: Making It Happen," McKinsey & Company Research, 2010. http://www.mckinsey.com/features/women_matter.

8   Barsh and Yee, "Unlocking the Full Potential of Women in the US Economy," supra.

9   Nancy M. Carter and Harvey M. Wagner, "The Bottom Line: Corporate Performance and Women's Representation on Boards (2004–2008)," Catalyst Research, March 2011, http://www.catalyst.org/knowledge/bottom-line-corporate-performance-and-womens-representation-boards-20042008.

10 "Average Stock Price of Gender Diverse Corporate Boards Outperform Those with No Women," Thomson Reuters, July 2013, http://thomsonreuters.com/press-releases/072013/Average-Stock-Price-of-Gender-Diverse-Corporate-Boards-Outperform-Those-with-No-Women.

11 John Gerzema, *The Athena Doctrine: How Women (And The Men Who Think Like Them) Will Rule The Future* (San Francisco: Jossey-Bass, 2013); Herb Greenberg, Ph.D., "The Qualities that Distinguish Women Leaders," Caliper, 2013, https://www.calipercorp.com/portfolio/the-qualities-that-distin-guish-women-leaders/.

12 Greenberg, ibid.; "Talent Management Best Practice Series: Women in Leadership," Korn/Ferry Institute, 2013, http://store.lominger.com/store/lominger/en_US/pd/ThemeID.2815600/productID.285243700?resid=Us27uQoydREAAH09uNIAAACW&rests=1389214648857.

13 Anita Woolley and Thomas Malone, "What Makes a Team Smarter? More Women," *Harvard Business Review,* June 2011, http://hbr.org/2011/06/defend-your-research-what-makes-a-team-smarter-more-women/ar/1 (If a group includes more women, its collective intelligence rises).

14 National Association of Women Business Owners, 2013, http://nawbo.org/section_103.cfm.

15 "Growing Under the Radar: An Exploration of the Achievements of Million-Dollar Women-Owned Firms," Report Commissioned by American Express OPEN, 2013, https://d8a8a12b527478184df8-1fd282026c3ff4ae711d11ecc95a1d47.ssl.cf1.rackcdn.com/wp-content/uploads/2013/07/GrowingUndertheRadar_Full-Report.pdf.

16 "A Current Glance at Women in the Law," American Bar Association Commission on Women in the Profession, February 2013, http://www.americanbar.org/content/dam/aba/marketing/women/current_glance_statistics_feb2013.authcheckdam.pdf.

17 Wendy Wang, Kim Parker and Paul Taylor, "Breadwinner Moms," Pew Research Center, May 29, 2013, http://www.pewsocialtrends.org/2013/05/29/breadwinner-moms/.

18 Cathy Benko and Bill Pelster, "How Women Decide," *Harvard Business Review*, September 2013, http://hbr.org/2013/09/how-women-decide/ (As a side benefit, Deloitte found that connections among colleagues inside the company also improved, accelerating the company's diversity efforts).

19 Jeffrey Pfeffer, *Managing with Power*, (Boston: Harvard Business School Press, 1994); Robert B. Cialdini, "Harnessing the Science of Persuasion," Harvard Business Review, October 2001, http://hbr.org/product/harnessing-the-science-of-persuasion/an/R0109D-PDF-ENG.

20 Sylvia Ann Hewlett, *The Sponsor Effect: Breaking Through the Last Glass Ceiling*, supra; Herminia Ibarra, Nancy M. Carver and Christine Silva, "Why Men Still Get More Promotions Than Women," *Harvard Business Review*, September 2010, http://hbr.org/2010/09/why-men-still-get-more-promotions-than-women/; Nancy M. Carter and Christine Silva, "Mentoring: Necessary But Insufficient for Advancement," Catalyst Research, 2010, http://www.catalyst.org/knowledge/mentoring-necessary-insufficient-advancement; Saadia Zahidi and Herminia Ibarra, "The Corporate Gender Gap," World Economic Forum, 2010, http://www.weforum.org/issues/corporate-gender-gap.

21 Carter and Silva, *Mentoring: Necessary But Insufficient for Advancement,* supra.

22 Joanna Barsh and Lareina Yee, "Changing companies' minds about women," *McKinsey Quarterly,* September 2011, http://www.mckinsey.com/insights/organization/changing_companies_minds_about_women.

23 "Women CEOs of the Fortune 1000," Catalyst Research, September 2013, http://www.catalyst.org/knowledge/women-ceos-fortune-1000; "Women in Senior Management: Setting the Stage for Growth," supra; 2012 Catalyst Census: Fortune 500 Women Executives and Top Earners, Catalyst Research, December 11, 2012, http://www.catalyst.org/knowledge/women-executive-officer-top-earners-fortune-500-0; Hewlett, *The Sponsor Effect,* supra.

24 Sara Randazzo, "Women Partner Watch 2013: Gaining Ground," *The American Lawyer,* October 1, 2013, http://www.americanlawyer.com/PubArticleTAL.jsp?id=1202584426718&slreturn=20140002184021.

25 "Report of the Seventh Annual NAWL National Survey on the Retention and Promotion of Women in Law Firms," NAWL Foundation, October 2012, http://www.nawl.org/p/cm/ld/fid=82.

26 "2013 Best Law Firms for Women Executive Summary," Working Mother Media & FlexTime Lawyers LLC, 2013, http://www.wmmsurveys.com/2013_WorkingMother_and_Flex-Time_Lawyers_BestLawFirms_for_Women_Executive_Summary.pdf.

27 Carter and Wagner, "The Bottom Line: Corporate Performance and Women's Representation on Boards (2004–2008)," supra; "We all mind the gap," Hay Group, July 2, 2013, http://www.thehrdirector.com/features/pay/we-all-mind-the-gap/; NAWL National Survey, supra; Jeffrey Lowe, "Partner Compensation Survey 2012," Major, Lindsey & Africa LLC, 2012, http://www.mlaglobal.com/~/media/Files/Allegis/MLAGlobal/Partner%20Compensation%20Survey/2012/FullReport.pdf; David Gaddis Ross, "Like Father, Like Daughter," Columbia Business School, February 22, 2011, http://www8.gsb.columbia.edu/ideas-at-work/publication/733/like-daughter-like-father.

28 Meghan Casserly, "Bad News from the Top: The Gender Pay Gap in the C-Suite Is Still Women's Fault," Forbes, August 13, 2013, http://www.forbes.com/sites/meghancasserly/2013/08/13/bad-news-from-the-top-the-gender-pay-gap-in-the-c-suite-is-still-womens-fault/.

29 Rebekah Mintzer, "Survey Finds High-Level Women In-House Lawyers Paid Less," Corporate Counsel, September 9, 2013, http://www.law.com/corporatecounsel/PubArticleCC.jsp?id=1202618551555.

30 Lowe, "Partner Compensation Survey 2012," supra.

31 Marina Angel, Eun-Young Whang, Rajiv D. Banker and Joseph Lopez, "Statistical Evidence on the Gender Gap in Law Firm Partner Compensation," Temple University Legal Studies Research Paper , September 9, 2010, http://papers.ssrn.com/sol3/papers.cfm?abstract_id=1674630.

32 Eileen Pollack, "Why Are There Still So Few Women in Science?," The New York Times Magazine, October 3, 2013, http://www.nytimes.com/2013/10/06/magazine/why-are-there-still-so-few-women-in-science.html?_r=0 ; Sylvia Ann Hewlett, et al., The Athena Factor: Reversing the Brain Drain in Science, Engineering, and Technology, HBR Research Materials, May 22, 2008, http://hbr.org/product/the-athena-factor-reversing-the-brain-drain-in-sci/an/10094-HCB-ENG.

33 "Women in STEM: A Gender Gap to Innovation: Executive Summary," U.S. Department of Commerce, August 2011, http://www.esa.doc.gov/sites/default/files/reports/documents/womeninstemagaptoinnovation8311.

pdf; Association for Women in Science, http://awis.org/displaycommon. cfm?an=1&subarticlenbr=519.

34 Sylvia Ann Hewlett, *(Forget a Mentor) Find a Sponsor,* supra.

35 Sponsors can learn a lot by taking the Implicit Association Test (IAT), which reveals biases and attitudes that they may not be consciously aware of and may even contradict their explicit behavior. https://implicit.harvard.edu/implicit/demo/.

36 Corinne A. Moss-Racusin, et al., "Science Faculty's Subtle Gender Biases Favor Male Students," Proceedings of the National Academy of Sciences of the United States of America, July 2012, http://www.pnas.org/content/109/41/16474.full. pdf+html.

37 Herminia Ibarra, Robin Ely and Deborah Kolb, "Women Rising: The Unseen Barriers," *Harvard Business Review,* September 2013, http://hbr.org/2013/09/women-rising-the-unseen-barriers/.

38 Joanna Barsh and Lareina Yee, "Unlocking the full potential of women at work," McKinsey & Company Research, 2012, http://www.mckinsey.com/careers/women/~/media/Reports/Women/2012%20WSJ%20Women%20in%20the%20Economy%20white%20paper%20FINAL.ashx; "Understanding Associates: New Perspectives on Associate Satisfaction and Morale," Hildebrandt International, 2007, http://www.thresholdadvisors.com/wp-content/uploads/2011/05/Pro-Bono-Associate-Article.pdf.

39 Eileen Patten and Kim Parker, "A Gender Reversal On Career Aspirations, Pew Research Social & Demographic Trends," April 2012, http://www.pewsocialtrends.org/2012/04/19/a-gender-reversal-on-career-aspirations/; also see "Edward Jones Survey Reveals 65 Percent of Americans Agree "Glass Ceiling" Remains as Career Barrier for Women," *The Wall Street Journal,* June 5, 2013, ote 39, http://online.wsj.com/article/PR-CO-20130605-907054.html.

40 "Women and Men in U.S. Corporate Leadership: Same Workplace, Different Realities?," Catalyst Research, 2004, http://www.catalyst.org/knowledge/women-and-men-us-corporate-leadership-same-workplace-different-realities.

41 Nancy M. Carter and Christine Silva, "The Myth of the Ideal Worker: Does Doing All the Right Things Really Get Women Ahead?," Catalyst, 2011, http://www.catalyst.org/knowledge/myth-ideal-worker-does-doing-all-right-things-really-get-women-ahead.

42 "Talent Management Best Practice Series: Women in Leadership," Korn/Ferry Institute, 2013, supra; Janice Fanning Madden, "Performance-Support Bias and the Gender Pay Gap Among Stockbrokers," *Gender & Society,* June 2012,

http://intl-gas.sagepub.com/content/26/3/488.abstract; Christine Silva, Nancy M. Carter and Anna Beninger, "Good Intentions, Imperfect Execution? Women Get Fewer of the 'Hot Jobs' Needed to Advance," Catalyst, November 2012, http://www.catalyst.org/knowledge/good-intentions-imperfect-execution-women-get-fewer-hot-jobs-needed-advance.

43 Eileen Pollack, supra.

44 Vivia Chen, "Associates Survey 2013: The Great (Gender) Divide," *The American Lawyer,* August 28, 2013, http://www.americanlawyer.com/PubArticleTAL.jsp?id=1202616217072.

45 "Talent Management Best Practice Series: Women in Leadership," Korn/Ferry Institute, 2013, supra.

46 Monica Biernat, M. J. Tocci and Joan C. Williams, "The Language of Performance Evaluations: Gender-Based Shifts in Content and Consistency of Judgment," *Social Psychological and Personality Science,* July 18 2011, http://spp.sagepub.com/content/early/2011/07/15/1948550611415693.

47 Marianne Cooper, "For Women Leaders, Likability and Success Hardly Go Hand-in-Hand," HBR Blog Network, April 30, 2013, http://blogs.hbr.org/2013/04/for-women-leaders-likability-a/.

48 Sylvia Ann Hewlett, *(Forget a Mentor) Find a Sponsor,* supra.

49 Kathleen Kelley Reardon, Ph.D., *The Secret Handshake: Mastering the Politics of the Business Inner Circle,* New York: Currency, 2001; McKinsey, "Unlocking the full potential of women," supra.

50 Ida O. Abbott, *Women on Top: The Woman's Guide to Leadership and Power in Law Firms,* Thomson Reuters, 2010, http://www.idaabbott.com/publications/books/women-top-womans-guide-leadership-and-power-law-firms.

51 Robert B. Cialdini, "Harnessing the Science of Persuasion," *Harvard Business Review,* October 2001, http://hbr.org/product/harnessing-the-science-of-persuasion/an/R0109D-PDF-ENG.

52 Shari L. Klevens and J. Randolph Evans, "'Billy Graham Rule' No Longer Suits Modern-Day Law Firms," *The Daily Report,* October 22, 2013, http://www.dailyreportonline.com/PubArticleDRO.jsp?id=1202624472959&slreturn=20140002204758.

53 Sylvia Ann Hewlett, *The Sponsor Effect,* supra.